KT-165-502

Making Meetings Work

'This is a great book...a short guide to making meetings work.' - TRAINING JOURNAL

Julie-Ann Amos

Second Edition

howtobooks

Practical books that inspire

You're in Charge Now!
The first-time manager's survival kit

Managing Difficult People
*Effective management strategies for handling
challenging behaviour*

Managing Your Time
What to do and how to do it in order to do more

Delegating
*Pass the right tasks on to the right people and
everyone will benefit*

Leading Teams
Delivering results through teamworking

howtobooks

Please send for a free copy of the latest catalogue:

HowTo Books
3 Newtec Place, Magdalen Road,
Oxford OX4 1RE, United Kingdom
info@howtobooks.co.uk
www.howtobooks.co.uk

Making
Meetings Work

Published by How To Books Ltd,
3 Newtec Place, Magdalen Road,
Oxford OX4 1RE. United Kingdom.
Tel: (01865) 793806. Fax: (01865) 248780.
info@howtobooks.co.uk
www.howtobooks.co.uk

All rights reserved. No part of this work may be reproduced
or stored in an information retrieval system (other than for
purposes of review) without the express permission of the
publisher in writing.

© Copyright 2002 Julie-Ann Amos

British Library Cataloguing in Publication Data.
A catalogue record for this book is available from
the British Library.

Cover design by Baseline Arts Ltd, Oxford
Produced for How To Books by Deer Park Productions
Typeset by PDQ Typesetting, Newcastle-under-Lyme, Staffs.
Printed and bound by Bell & Bain Ltd, Glasgow

NOTE: The material contained in this book is set out in good faith for general guidance and no liability can be accepted for loss or expense incurred
as a result of relying in particular circumstances on statements made in
the book. Laws and regulations are complex and liable to change, and read-
ers should check the current position with the relevant authorities before
making personal arrangements.

Contents

Preface

Most people have experienced a poor meeting. They waste time, cost money, and can stir up ill feeling, frustration and interpersonal conflict.

Handled well, however, meetings can be invaluable tools for getting things agreed, discussed and taken forward. An understanding of how meetings work and how to improve them is therefore essential for anyone who holds or attends a lot of meetings.

If you chair or lead a meeting, there is a great deal you can do to make it productive. But even if you are attending someone else's meeting, you can still steer the meeting towards being better without taking over.

This book takes you through meetings from preparation to the actions necessary afterwards. It will help just about anyone make better use of their meetings.

Enjoyable meetings that are productive and help to get the job required done are an ideal that *is* possible with a little work.

Julie-Ann Amos

Acknowledgement

This book is dedicated to Mr Ritchie Stevenson, one of the greatest mentors I have had. Much of the material in it comes from him, or was devised jointly between us during our time working together.

I am indebted to him for the knowledge, wisdom and advice he imparted over our six years together, on this and other subjects.

I can only hope this book is as good as he would expect.

1 · Introduction

Meetings could and should be an efficient tool to assist you in getting decisions, information and action agreed and instigated.

In this Chapter:

1 THE COST OF MEETINGS

2 TAKING RESPONSIBILITY

3 RETHINK YOUR MEETINGS

4 WHY MEETINGS FAIL

Meetings can take over your life. By the time you've attended the regular team/group meetings you usually go to, plus meetings about specific projects or tasks, plus any special meetings to deal with the 'out of the ordinary', many of us have precious little time to actually work.

What is it about meetings that we find so interesting that we spend half our lives in them? Nothing, of course! We just end up being caught in a cycle of more and more meetings, run less and less efficiently, with poor chairing, taking up an ever-increasing amount of time and achieving little. No wonder so many people dread meetings.

For many of us, meetings have become a way of life. We need to rethink, so we only attend the meetings we really need to, spend as little time as possible there, achieving as much as we can — both at the meeting and as a result of it.

IS THIS YOU?

- I love meetings! They get me out of the office and away from the blasted paperwork.

- Meetings are frustrating — I never get a chance to say what I think. Everyone just goes along with the majority and one voice can't be heard anyway.

- These meetings would be fine if I could run them. With *her* in charge, they ramble on for hours going nowhere.

■ If I want to be bossed about, I'll go back to school! Who do they think they are? Just because they're chairing the meeting doesn't give them the right to speak to us like that!

■ Our meetings are great. They're amicable, and everyone has their say. We make major decisions and always get consensus. But then no-one ever seems to *do* anything. The same things come up again and again.

1 · THE COST OF MEETINGS

How productive are meetings?

How many times have you caught someone (or even your-self) doing one of the following in a meeting:

■ daydreaming
■ doodling
■ doing other work they have brought with them
■ dozing
■ making an excuse to leave.

How did things get so bad?

Because meetings are generally speaking pretty poor, many people have never experienced a truly efficient, productive meeting. Therefore, a lot of people don't realise their meetings are so appalling, or if they do, they don't recognise the importance of doing something about it. It's more convenient to continue as normal, and not try to change the ways things are done, so inertia is another reason why improvements never get made. For many people, it is simply too much time and effort to change the way they do things, despite the fact that the rewards are many and will save considerable time and effort in the end.

The impact of poor meetings

The simple by-product of poor meetings is lack of productivity. The worse the meeting is, the more tempting it is to give in to one of the above, and the worse the meeting gets, encouraging others to follow suit. Lack of productivity costs time and money. In time terms, meetings end up being longer than necessary, and so generate fewer results. You need more meetings therefore, to achieve objectives. Spending time in the meetings means other work doesn't get done, which causes frustration. It's a vicious circle.

Things look even bleaker when you consider the cost in monetary terms, rather than in time. Meetings are expensive. Very often it is the senior people in an organisation, and therefore those more highly paid, who attend the most meetings. *Wall Street Journal* published some figures which are often quoted about meetings and how much time is spent in them:

- The average chief executive officer, 17 hours per week.
- Average senior executive, 23 hours per week.
- Average middle managers, 11 hours per week.

What is worse, the managers researched said that only 56 per cent of their meetings were productive, and over 25 per cent could have been replaced with a simple memo or telephone call.

Just think of the cost to an organisation – those people could be *working*. If 15 hours was a rough average per week to spend in meetings (and it is for a lot of office workers), and a person works an average of 45 hours a week, that's a third of his or her time in meetings. So one third of their salary pays for meetings, the other two thirds go towards actually getting their job done.

Take this a stage further: say each meeting has six people in it, that third of their salaries is equivalent to no meetings, but employing two extra staff. How much more could *you* get done at work with two extra people? Remember, that's two extra people *per set of six people spending one third of their week in meetings*. No wonder organisations are short staffed – they're spending all their time in meetings.

The cost of meetings is very high as can be seen from the figures below. To calculate how much time y*ou* could be wasting in meetings, take one of your typical meetings, take the total approximate salaries of the people attending the meeting, and add up the cost of that meeting based on how long it took. If you assume an eight hour working day and 260 working days a year, you should be able to calculate the cost of any meeting. Surprising how it mounts up, isn't it?

Approx annual salary total of attendees £	Cost per hour £	Cost per half hour £	Cost per quarter hour £
200,000	96.15	48.08	24.04
150,000	72.12	36.06	18.03
125,000	60.10	30.05	15.02
100,000	48.08	24.04	12.02
90,000	43.27	21.63	10.82
80,000	38.46	19.23	9.62
70,000	33.65	16.83	8.41
60,000	28.85	14.42	7.21
50,000	24.04	12.02	6.01
40,000	19.23	9.62	4.81

Figures based on 260 working days per year, 8 hours per day

Just one unnecessary person at a meeting, or one extra quarter hour wasted can be a horrific cost over a year. There are other costs too:

- Sales or production lost whilst staff are in a meeting.
- Other work not getting done.
- Missed opportunity ('opportunity costs').
- Lost efficiency as people get frustrated, demodulated or strained in their working relationships.
- Consequences of delays.
- Attention diverted from other important tasks.

'Would your boss let you spend £100 an hour on getting advice on this project? Not likely! So why is it OK to spend £100 an hour in meetings discussing it?'

2 · TAKING RESPONSIBILITY

Take responsibility for the meetings you attend – whether or not you chair them. Someone has to, and if it isn't the person who's chairing, it might as well be you. Regardless of what role you play, here's how to take responsibility for a meeting. You may be on your own, but at least one person there will be effective and efficient, and hopefully others might follow your lead eventually.

- Prepare – take along any data, facts or information you need, including all relevant papers.

- Read things beforehand if asked to, or even if not, if you think it might help.

- Be clear and concise.

- Don't talk unless you have good reason. Arguing or interrupting is *never* a good reason.

- Know when to give in. If no one is supporting you, further discussion is pointless. Know when to retire gracefully, and don't sulk about it.

- Take things further if you really feel the meeting is wrong and you are right – but do it outside the meeting to save other people's time.

- Cancel unnecessary meetings, or explain why you won't be attending.

- Action agreed tasks after the meeting.

- Make notes of decisions taken or tasks allocated.

- Respect people and their opinions. Assist anyone having a hard time getting heard.

- Arrive and finish on time.

There are plenty more things we could list here, but this is a start, and the rest of the book will expand on specific ways you can manage your meetings.

> *'Even if you're the only one there that behaves responsibly, at least you have a clear conscience and no frustration when you leave. That's more than a lot of people achieve at a meeting.'*

3 · RETHINK YOUR MEETINGS

Good meetings are for good reason(s)

The objective of a meeting should never be to have a

meeting. That may sound silly, but it's surprising how often it happens. Meetings are a means to an end, never an end. There are many reasons for a meeting. Here are just a few:

- Briefing people.
- Exchanging information.
- Negotiating a deal.
- Making decisions.
- Talking things through.
- Resolving conflict.
- Establishing a plan.
- Regular sessions to do a combination of the above.

What's in a name?

Very often we hold or attend meetings which serve a number of purposes. This is a good way of saving time, but can also mean that people become confused about the purpose of the meeting. Try to give each meeting a purpose, even if this is no more than 'Regular weekly team meeting'. People then know why the meeting is being held.

Meetings called 'sales targets' or similar ambiguous names make people unsure why the meeting is being held. Is this to *discuss* sales targets? To *set* them? To *agree* them? To *give opinions* so that the Sales Director can set them? Or even to *review* past performance against last quarter's sales targets? People can only be prepared and come to the meeting in the right mindset if they know *why* they are attending.

Many problems arise because people *think* they are at a meeting to do one thing, but others (possibly including the meeting leader or chair) are under the impression they are there to do something else.

For example, you call a meeting to consult your team about an important change you're thinking of making – say, compulsory weekend working. You call it 'Weekend working meeting'. The team get very worked up; it's an emotive subject. Some are in favour, whereas others will be badly affected by the potential change and will argue very strongly against. Some people will arrive unprepared, as they don't want to work weekends, and think the meeting is to discuss volunteering for this, rather than compulsory working. They will be angry or upset when they realise they have misunderstood.

This meeting is a recipe for disaster. Why? Because you've not told people the purpose. Unless everyone at that meeting knows they are only there to be consulted because you will make a decision afterwards, there will be a lot of unnecessary argument and conflict. People will think this is their only opportunity to have their say or influence the decision. Personalities will clash, and personal relationships may be broken in ways that will take a long time to heal.

Another example would be where people attend a meeting and are asked to make decisions, when they haven't had a chance to think the issues through – they thought they were simply there to discuss or to be consulted. Very often in this case, people will resent being asked to decide, so debate will go on and on. These type of meetings can often end up spending a great deal of time making a decision about whether or not they can and should decide at the meeting, rather than deciding the decision itself.

Discontinue unnecessary meetings

If you find you can't state the purpose of a meeting easily, and that it's simply a regular event, ask yourself and others whether or not you need to continue with them.

Timing and meetings

Sometimes, killing two birds with one stone is not the best thing to do. Think about whether splitting a meeting into two shorter meetings would be a better idea. Or if you do need one long meeting, consider having a break at 'half time' – this can keep participants fresh, focused and on track.

Attention spans are not infinite. On average, people can pay attention for only about 20 minutes without becoming restless. Even a change in speaker or topic can bring things back on track and refocus attention on the matter in hand.

If a meeting lasts for more than an hour there needs to be a break. It's counterproductive to keep grinding on without one, as attention spans cannot be re-energised by a new topic too often without a proper break.

Another consideration is *when* to meet.

- Don't meet first thing on a Monday morning — most people need time to get into the swing of the working week.

- Don't meet immediately after lunch — people are in post-lunch nap mode.

- Don't meet late on a Friday afternoon — people are more focused on the weekend than the business in hand.

'Many meetings don't have a clear purpose or outcome. Having a firm idea about why you are there can help enormously in making it happen, and prevent sidetracking into things that take time away from the meeting's purpose.'

4 · WHY MEETINGS FAIL

Often, meetings don't fail due to deliberate action, but because misunderstanding or coincidence gets in the way. Here are some reasons why meetings can fail. These are 'diseases' of meetings, and it can be helpful to recognise the 'symptoms'.

- **Interruptions and disruptions**. Noisy rooms and interruptions such as mobile phones and messages, people arriving late or departing early – these all disrupt meetings.

- **Lack of focus**. No purpose for meetings, no goal to achieve. Not knowing what the objective is – and not asking for one.

- **Unclear purpose**. Meetings where participants are under the mistaken impression they are there for a different purpose than intended. People want to talk about aspects of the issue that aren't relevant. Discussion wanders onto other subjects.

- **Objective not achieved**. Decisions not taken. People say they need more time. Information given was inadequate or not understood.

- **Politics/interpersonal motives are brought in**. Meetings become confrontational. Participants 'gang up' on each other. One or more people try to manipulate the meeting. Hidden agendas are in operation.

- **Poor (or lack of) preparation**. People don't have the right facts or information with them. Research hasn't been done. Papers sent out haven't been read.

- **Poor chairing/leadership**. Either chairing the meeting like a military general, with no flexibility and everyone afraid to speak up, or weak chairing, so the meeting is taken over by participants. In between these two extremes, poor control can lead to meandering discussions, allowing open confrontationl, lax discipline and standards, people reading, starting private side conversations, lateness, etc. Most problems could be cured with the perfect chair in control of a meeting.

- **Poor environment**. Eight people crammed into a room big enough for three. A table covered with tea and coffee cups and no room for papers. Or three people at one end of an enormous conference table. Noisy rooms, meetings in open plan offices, hot stuffy meeting rooms, or freezing cold school halls. Do any of these sound familiar?

- **Poor timing**. Meetings starting late. People arriving late. Meetings overrunning. Meetings finishing with only part of the agenda completed. Meetings scheduled at times when participants can ill-afford to be away from their work, e.g. end of month meetings for accountants. Meetings scheduled before necessary information is ready or available (a recipe for a pointless talking shop) or too late to influence decisions.

- **Right people absent**. People with necessary input or information not invited or not available. Unexpected no-shows. Fifteen minutes wasted at the start phoning round reminding people they should be in attendance and the meeting has started. Meetings abandoned because critical people don't show up.

- **Sabotage**. People deliberately trying to manipulate the meeting. Participants with a grudge or disagreement with the chair or another participant. People with hidden agendas trying to manipulate the meetings towards their own desired outcome.

■ **Unnecessary meetings**. Meetings 'because we have one every week'. Meetings to give a simple message that could have been an email or memo. Meetings to get feedback on an idea which could have been sent out for written feedback. Meetings when there's nothing on the agenda but regular items. Meetings to report back on matters decided or arranged at the last meeting.

■ **Wrong people present**. Just as having the right people absent can ruin a meeting, having the wrong people present can have the same effect. People who don't want or need to be there can be disruptive without even meaning to be. People who have no knowledge of matters being discussed can draw out proceedings, asking questions unnecessarily.

> *'Knowing why meetings fail is part of the battle. You can't do anything about a problem unless you know the cause.'*

IN SUMMARY

■ Make people realise how much meetings cost – it's surprising how they will talk less and achieve things more quickly.

■ Take responsibility for a meeting whoever is chairing, but do it tactfully. You can still influence and keep a meeting on track if someone else is running it – without them losing face.

■ Rethink your meetings asking why you are attending them, or why you are holding the meeting. Ask yourself (and others if necessary) every time – 'What's the purpose of this meeting?'

■ Understand what goes wrong in a meeting and why, and it will help you see how to help prevent it happening again.

2 · Planning and Preparation

'Why is it we never prepare properly for meetings? It would make life so much easier.'

In this Chapter:

Very often, it's easy to point at something that happens in a meeting and say, 'that's the problem'. Yet most of these problems can be solved, avoided or reduced by preparation and planning.

Most of us don't prepare adequately for meetings, and it's usually caused by a lack of time. Preparation time, however, is time *invested* rather than spent. It can easily be recouped when the meeting is shorter as a consequence, and sometimes it means that you save time in every meeting of that group in future.

Not preparing and planning definitely increases the amount of time we spend (waste) in meetings. This means taking a little time to read when necessary. Also, giving proper thought to who to invite, and structuring the agenda accordingly.

A little time given to considering what *might* happen or go wrong may often prevent it by helping you to think ahead.

IS THIS YOU?

■ I have to go to all these meetings purely because *someone* from my section has to. Half the time they don't even ask me anything.

■ We have meetings to discuss every single issue. Why doesn't the boss just put them all together and have one big meeting every couple of weeks?

■ By the time I get the agenda, I've no time to query it. Half the time I don't even look at it – it doesn't tell me much anyway.

■ We get a great pack of paper with the agenda and minutes, then spend the first 20 minutes having it read to us. What's the point?

■ I hate these meetings! Everybody rambles on endlessly – we could get twice as much done with half the people.

1 · IS A MEETING NECESSARY?

Here are some reasons people hold meetings that can be unnecessary.

■ **Finding out what's happening**. These meetings are fine for you, as everyone tells you what their department is doing. But they all have to sit through each other's information. If you alone need to know what everyone is doing, ask them individually or schedule one-on-ones.

■ **You need a quick decision**. If you can get everyone together quickly, this can be a good use of a meeting. However, it will take far longer for say, six people to decide something than two or three. Consider having a smaller meeting of key people to speed up discussion and decision-making.

■ **The weekly/monthly/quarterly meeting**. One boss insisted on daily meetings with his management team, and these morning meetings usually took one and a half to two hours. That was a large percentage of everyone's day which could have used more productively. Regular meetings can be good or bad – schedule them at the right frequency. Is weekly too frequent, for example? Never be afraid to skip one. If there's not a lot going to change or happening, cancel the next meeting and hold issues over until the one after.

■ **You want to keep everyone involved**. Telling people decisions you've made isn't involving them, it's informing them. If you don't need their input, don't ask for it. Raising expectations that they can influence something is unfair. Instead, send an email or memo to say what is happening and why, and invite questions.

■ **Passing on non-controversial information**. This is more quickly and easily done by memo or email. Don't waste time having a meeting.

> *'Don't have meetings unless they are necessary. That sounds obvious, but more to the point, try to avoid attending other people's meetings unless your presence is necessary.'*

2 · WHO TO INVITE – THE PARTICIPANTS

Consider inviting people who fulfil the following criteria to your meeting wherever possible.

People who need to give approval

All too often we have a meeting and then take the results to someone else for approval. Consider having them there to hear views first hand – unless you can easily get hold of them afterwards for approval.

People with expertise/experience

Invite people with directly relevant expertise or experience to give you input or answer questions. That way, if you need input, you don't have to go away and then have another meeting to feed back their information, or call another meeting with them there.

People with creativity or intelligence

These people will help a group generate ideas and/or discussion. But beware – these people may become disruptive if they have too little to do in a long meeting.

People who will carry out decisions

If someone will be responsible for carrying out a decision made at the meeting, try to have them there. That way, they understand fully all the reasons and background to the actions required of them, and usually, people do a better job if they have been involved in decision-making about it. However, if they don't need or expect to be involved in the decision-making, it is acceptable to leave them out.

People who will support you

This is a difficult one. Sometimes it is tempting or necessary to draft in extra support. But it may be obvious that this is why people are present, and it may make others suspicious or more hostile, so invite your supporters with care.

> *'Always try to invite the right people to make life easier for you.'*

3 · WHO NOT TO INVITE

Try to avoid inviting people who will be unhelpful, or who will not assist you in moving the meeting forward.

People who generally exhibit unhelpful behaviour

Some people just seem to be permanently difficult. They can be very hard to control, even impossible at times. Try to exclude these people wherever possible, and they may even appreciate it. But be careful – don't exclude people who will be even more difficult if excluded.

People who don't want or need to be there

These people often get frustrated. But if you have your own reasons for them being there, fine – just make sure you let them know why they're needed.

Too many people

Unless they all absolutely have to be present, always take care not to invite so many people that the meeting becomes difficult and time-consuming.

People invited out of courtesy/political protocol

It is better to try to convince them of the time they will save by not attending.

People who don't need to be there for the whole meeting

Unless there is no practical way of determining that someone won't be needed for another issue, invite them for their agenda item, then let them (and make them) leave.

> *'Who to invite and who not to invite is important to the success of a meeting. Getting it wrong can be devastating in terms of outcome, as well as wasting people's time.'*

4 · BACKGROUND INFORMATION

Sending out background information

When confirming the date and time of a meeting, it is usual to send out an agenda if more than one issue is to be raised. At the same time, you can send out any background information. Consider:

- What information you can give people before the meeting to save time going through it. For example, briefing documentation.

- Whether anyone needs special information, such as notes or briefing about a previous meeting.

- Whether you want people to take any action before the meeting. For example, to gain opinions from colleagues or clients.

- Whether you should pre-brief one or two people about an issue in order to enlist/ensure their support.

Receiving background information

- Read it! Or, at least look through it to see whether you *should* read it.

- Make notes of anything you want clarified, or any questions you want to raise.

- Note any points you want to make.

- Use the information to decide whether you really need to attend the meeting or not. Very often the background information is useful enough to help you decide that you no longer need to attend.

Other tips

When chairing a meeting, never spend time going through information you have sent out beforehand. It lets people know they can get away without going through it. Always assume they have read it, and let them be disadvantaged if they haven't. It's not your job to look after people. If necessary, have a short break whilst they go through it and then reconvene. Give them the message you won't accommodate poor preparation.

> *'Very few people actually do anything with background information sent out before meetings. Not going through it is just a waste of paper, and someone obviously thought you needed it.'*

5 · CREATING AN AGENDA

When thinking about calling a meeting, you should first determine what needs to be covered and then consider how best to cover those items. Too often these decisions are ignored, with disastrous consequences. Agendas are something very often produced, seldom stuck to, and more often than not, of little use. A good agenda will revolutionise your meetings.

What to include in an agenda

Most people use an agenda to:

■ Give the start time of the meeting and location.

■ List participants expected to attend.

■ List issues / items to be raised.

■ Give the order in which they will be dealt with.

■ Announce who will be leading or handling each issue – usually by putting a name by any item to be handled by a particular individual. For example:

1   Sales figures (John).
2   Overtime (Simon).

Other uses of an agenda

There are, however, other uses:

■ State the purpose of the meeting.

■ Indicate expected outcomes – each agenda item could show the purpose of that item.

■ Place a time limit on each topic – stopping indefinite discussion and later items being rushed or not dealt with at all.

■ Indicate the finishing time of the meeting – giving all participants light at the end of the tunnel, and an idea of how little time they have to waste on time-consuming issues.

How to send out an agenda

■ Send a note or email stating:
  – there will be a meeting
  – the purpose
  – the administrative details, such as when and where it will be held
  – ask those invited to accept or decline the meeting

- make it clear that once they have accepted, they are expected to attend
- ask anyone with an agenda item to contact you before
  the meeting with their request and the amount of time
  they will need to present it (and give a deadline for
  doing so).

■ Deal with any inappropriate requests for agenda items – suggest the item be discussed in another meeting

■ Send the agenda to all the meeting participants with a reminder of the meeting's purpose, location, time and duration.

■ Chapter 3 deals with the intricacies of agendas in more detail,
and how to use them to effectively control a meeting.

> *'Agendas can be hugely effective in organising and
> streamlining meetings, but are rarely used
> effectively.'*

6 · ANTICIPATING AND PREVENTING PROBLEMS

Keeping meetings to time

Your meetings often start late and run over time, but it doesn't have to be this way. It's time to take your meetings more seriously. Whether you're the meeting organiser or the attendee, commit to starting and finishing your meetings on time. Expect attendees to be punctual and the meeting to finish on schedule. Intolerance for tardiness will set a behavioural standard for the group, and participants will likely conform if expectations are well-defined and consistently enforced. Listed below are some tips to help you and your group stay on time.

Timing for meeting organisers

■ State that the meeting will begin promptly at the scheduled time and that all participants should be on time.

■ Send a reminder email thirty minutes before the meeting begins and encourage meeting participants to arrive on time.

■ Ensure that you begin the meeting at the scheduled time. If you've encouraged others to be prompt, don't embarrass yourself by showing up late.

■ Close the meeting room doors at the scheduled time, and start. There's nothing like late attendees to disrupt the flow of a meeting.

■ If your meeting starts a little late, you should still aim to finish the meeting at the scheduled time. It's inconsiderate to assume the participants' diaries revolve around you and your meeting, so finish when you promised you would.

■ Consider creating a 'latecomer jar' to which meeting participants must contribute each time they arrive late.

Timing for meeting attendees

■ Quickly review the agenda before heading to the meeting. Remind yourself why you're attending.

■ Make your way to the meeting ten minutes before it actually begins. This will give you enough time for a trip to the loo, to speak to anyone you bump into along the way, pour a cup of coffee or deal with any last minute emergencies before you leave.

■ Consider speaking up if the meeting organiser is late. If they consistently arrive ten minutes late, ask if it would be more convenient to start 15 minutes later next week.

■ Try to ask only relevant questions during the meeting. If your comment isn't directly related to the topic at hand, don't mention it.

■ Politely leave the meeting when it was scheduled to end. If meetings consistently overrun, this is a polite way to point this out.

You can be prepared for timing problems with a little forethought. It can really pay you at times to be just a little devious and manipulating, with good intent.

Problem people

If you know some people will be awkward, plan ahead. Think about what they might say and do, and prepare a course of action.

Hot topics

If some items will be controversial, think carefully about how to handle them. Consider the timing of these items in the agenda (see Chapter 3). Consider alliances and gaining support beforehand. If you know there will be opposition, prepare a good argument to counteract it.

Alliances and politics

Some people will strike alliances – always siding with each other, always supporting each other, always arguing or opposing certain people. Try to split them up – by ensuring they sit apart, or by excluding one person from the meeting.

Support

Who said you can't strike some alliances yourself? Call on one or two people to gain support before the meeting. Tell them why you're talking to them and that you would like some help.

The pre-emptive strike

If you know things will be difficult, try a surprise tactic to take the wind out of people's sails. Consider the following pre-emptive strikes:

- 'As you know I'm biased in favour of this. So I'd like to ask Stephanie to take over chairing the meeting so I don't influence it in any way.'

- 'Sarah, why don't you kick off on this topic? I know you have strong opinions, so let's hear you out first.'

- 'Sorry to interrupt, Gavin, but as we're limited for time, can we all restrict ourselves to two minutes on this topic? If you'd like to sum up . . .'

- 'It's obvious we aren't going to gain agreement today. Let's make a list of points in favour and against, and I'll refer this up the line.'

- 'I can see you all have a great many reservations. Let's write them down and prioritise them so I can discuss them with senior management.'

- 'Look, I hate these meetings as much as you do. So why don't we all try to get along and get this over with quickly so we can return to work?'

There are numerous others, but this gives you the general idea. Of course, any of them may backfire on you – they carry risk. For example, in the first idea, people may decide Stephanie is a better chair than you and they'd rather she took over running the meeting. But you can at least consider possible pre-emptive strikes as part of your preparation.

'A little thinking ahead can prevent disaster. Meetings have many participants, so unpleasantness and loss of face is public, and therefore can be more humiliating.'

IN SUMMARY

■ Is your meeting or attendance really necessary? Why?

■ Invite the right people, and let them know why it's important they attend.

■ Try to exclude the wrong people if at all possible.

■ Send out background information and expect people to use it. Use any you receive to decide whether you really need to attend.

■ Create an effective agenda, and stick to it. Be aware of how crucial it can be to a good meeting.

■ Prepare ideas for dealing with potential problems. Don't rehearse a rigid script – that never works. Just think things through and identify potential difficulties and ways of dealing with them.

3 · The Agenda

A good agenda can do half your work for you before the meeting even starts.

In this Chapter:

Few people read meeting agendas thoroughly. There is good reason for this – there's rarely any point. Few people make their agendas sufficiently informative for them to tell anyone anything other than the time and place of the meeting and the order in which issues will be raised.

No wonder most people just glance at the agenda and mentally count the number of items. Setting a good, informative agenda will make meetings much easier as people know what the items will be, why they are being included, and what action the meeting is hoping to take about each one.

A really good agenda even tells people how long the meeting will take and how much time will be devoted to each item. With an agenda like this, people reading it will be prepared for your meeting without even having to try.

IS THIS YOU?

- We raise the same issues every month. The agenda's just a waste of paper, so we stopped sending it out.

- I never read the agenda. It's just a list of topics, and I know what comes up each time.

- I know how to write an agenda. You start with the minutes of the last meeting, and end with any other business and put the items in between. There's no skill in that.

■ I'm so busy I don't have time to write a proper agenda as such – I'm in and out of meetings half the time as it is – I'd buy shares in the paper industry if we produced agendas for each one.

■ You only produce agendas for formal meetings, don't you?

1 · ASSESSING ITEMS

Always be realistic in terms of how much you can put into a meeting.

Encourage input

Ask people if they have any items for the agenda. At the end of a meeting, ask whether people have anything they'd like on the agenda for the next one. Just because it's your meeting, it doesn't mean you're the only one who needs to raise items – you can avoid surprises raised at the end under 'any other business' or 'any questions' by getting input for the agenda, giving you time to prepare.

Assess the purpose

There are only three reasons for putting an item on an agenda:

- To **inform**.
- To **discuss**.
- To **decide**.

Any issue will fall into one of these categories. Each item potentially on an agenda should be considered to see which category it falls into, and the agenda worded accordingly. For example:

1 Budget overspend (information from Roger).
2 Weekend working – discussion (all).
3 New rota – decision on attached proposal (from Sarah).

This makes it clear to everyone *why* you are including each item, and they can prepare for say, items 2 and/or 3, for example.

Assess importance

You can't have a limitless list of items that never gets completed – it's demoralising. Meetings will be more pleasant and stimulating if you get through the list each time, giving everyone the feeling the meeting achieves something.

Assess which items are most important and prioritise. You may have to go back to someone and ask if his or her item can wait until a future date.

*'Ask yourself for each agenda item – **why** are we including this? It might not be obvious to everyone.'*

2 · STANDARD ITEMS

Any agenda will usually, and should, contain standard items. It is common for agendas to conform the following pattern:

1 Minutes of the last meeting.

2 Apologies for absence.

3 Item.

4 Item.

5 Item, etc.

6 Any other business.

7 Date and time of the next meeting.

This is acceptable, but can lead to several problems. First, there's no incentive to arrive on time, if all that the first 5–10 minutes will consist of is someone going through the minutes from last time.

Secondly, item 2 gives a message that non-attendance is acceptable. Yet if you've invited all the right people to the meeting, you *need* them all to be there, so don't assume someone might be absent and give them the chance.

Item 6 also gives people an opportunity to raise items unexpectedly. Ideally, you'd like them to tell you of these in advance. It also prevents you from controlling the length of the meeting. Tell people items need to be given to you in advance, or raised without warning in real emergencies only.

The standard items might be changed slightly as follows:

1 Questions/issues from last meeting.
2 Changes to agenda – (only included if there are any).
3 Item.
4 Item.
5 Item, etc.
6 Further items (time permitting).
   a) Sickness Rates (Jonathan).
   b) Staff charity raffle (Sally).
7 Date and time of next meeting.

> *'Controlling the agenda enables you better control of the meeting, plus it allows people to prepare by putting them in the right mindset – without them even realising.'*

3 · ORDER

What order should the agenda items go in? This is where manipulation can really be used by the chair of the meeting to good effect. Strategies for deciding order include:

■ Most important first – which gets the most important things done first, but then 'win/lose' mentality may affect people, and those who lose may be awkward over less important issues later.

■ Least important first – which gives a good excuse/reason for not allowing much time to be spent on trivial items, but runs the risk of the important items not being completed.

■ Items only affecting one or two people first – so they can leave immediately after they are finished, saving their time.

■ Contentious 'hot topics' at the end – to reduce time available for them, but people can get frustrated and irritable during the previous items.

■ Routine matters first to get them out of the way.

■ Routine matters last – as you can issue an email or memo, should the meeting not have time for them.

As you can see, there are lots of ways to structure the order of items, and no answer is necessarily right or wrong. You alone know the issues and how the participants may feel about topics and consequently how they are likely to behave.

> *'Manipulating meetings can be done by something as simple as controlling the agenda – especially the order of items.'*

4 · TIMING

You can now go through the agenda, and allocate timing to each item. You know the start and finish time of the meeting, and can allocate time sensibly, based on how long you feel each item might take.

There is no harm in making this information public – when

the agenda goes out, let people know how long has been allocated to each item. If you are uneasy doing this, then send out an untimed agenda, but have an agenda with the item timings on it prepared for distribution at the start of the meeting.

Why show timings?

■ Keeps the meeting on track.

■ Lets everyone know time is limited.

■ Psychologically hints that behaviour such as long discussion on favourite topics is discouraged.

■ Provides a 'guillotine' – a mechanism for stopping a discussion – if ultimately necessary.

■ Gives you more control.

■ Motivates people – they know long pointless debate is unlikely.

■ Gives goals which can be accomplished, giving everyone a sense of achievement.

Open-ended meetings

These are meetings with a set start time but no finish time. A typical example would be school Board of Governors' meetings, which typically take place in the evening. People often feel 'stuck in them' for as long as they take, with no way out. Published finished times give people a goal to aim for, and everyone knows there is 'light at the end of the tunnel' in a difficult meeting.

If necessary, you can request an extension if the meeting is going slower than planned, but try not to do this on a regular basis, or people will come to see the published finish time as irrelevant.

'Give people deadlines – for the meeting and each item. It helps you control the meeting unobtrusively once this system is established as common practice.'

5 · WRITING THE AGENDA

Don't forget other people's items

When you send invitations to attend a meeting, it's customary to ask attendees if they have any agenda item requests. If you don't, people will often just suggest things anyway. If participants are able to contribute to the meeting agenda, they're more likely to feel positive and committed about attending the meeting. If there isn't room for someone's item, do discuss it with them, don't just cut it from the agenda, or you may invite trouble at the meeting itself.

Sending out the agenda

Having chosen your items for the agenda, assessed the order you would like them in, and allocated an approximate estimate of the time to be spent on each one, all you have to do is write the agenda out and send it to the participants.

Also include:

■ Any special requirements/instructions/notices, such as no smoking, lunch provided, mobiles off, no interruptions.

■ A brief description of each item in (at most) 3 or 4 lines.

■ A clear indication of any preparation needed.

An example agenda is on page 67.

Item 3 in particular is worth noting: Items 3 and 4 would be combined in most agendas, and this is obviously a 'hot topic' which will be contentious and arouse a lot of strong feeling and debate. By separating the presentation of information from Head Office and the consequent debate it causes, you effectively make space for the presentation of the information *before* people start to get into heated discussions. Just presenting the agenda in this way should prompt people to listen first, then debate, rather than just launching in.

Item 6 shows that feedback has been requested from staff on the new canteen arrangements. This is a memory-jog to anyone who hasn't already done this to do so before the meeting. This will be discussed, but by saying, 'consult', it's clear that any decisions to be made will be made outside the meeting, not at the meeting itself. Similarly with item 7

WEEKLY TEAM MEETING

MEETING ROOM 1

WEDNESDAY 3 MAY 200X, 1000-1130 a.m.

Chairperson – Tom Campbell, General Manager

ITEM	PURPOSE	RESPONSIBLE	TIME
1. Questions/issues arising from last meeting	Discussion	All	5 mins
2. Update on activities since last week – brief updates from each team (with figures e.g. budget and sales forecasts to hand out where appropriate for information, please)	Information	All	15 mins
3. New staffing structure proposals – information from Head Office regarding proposed changes	Information	Tom	10 mins
4. Discussion on 3 and formulation of questions/objections to be referred back to Head Office	Discussion	All (Tom to collate)	30 mins
5. Request from Accounts – new payments authorisation processes	Decision	Jeffrey	5 mins
6. Feedback from staff on new canteen arrangements	Consult	All – Ross to co-ordinate	15 mins
7. Staff party – arrangements	Consult	Tom/All	5 mins
8. Arrangements/items for the next meeting	Consult	Tom	5 mins

– don't let people think they are making a decision (which can change the way they discuss things and how co-operative they are) if the decision will not be taken at the meeting.

> *'If you have thought through the individual items carefully, the agenda will write itself.'*

IN SUMMARY

■ Assess each agenda item carefully for purpose – *why* is it necessary at that meeting?

■ Set up standard items that suit your particular meetings.

■ The order of items on the agenda is a way of manipulating the meeting for your own ends, to ensure maximum effectiveness and efficiency, and to minimise or eliminate time-wasting activities.

■ Give each item a proposed time limit. This will make your meetings more streamlined, and discourage time wasting.

■ Send out the agenda with a clear explanation of each item, who it involves, why it is on the agenda, and any necessary work to be done beforehand. Consider adding timings.

4 · Chairing Meetings

You don't know just how difficult it is to run a meeting until you try it yourself.

In this Chapter:

1 PLANNING AND PREPARATION

2 INTRODUCTIONS

3 DISCUSSION AND PARTICIPATION

4 HANDLING CONFLICT

5 GAINING AGREEMENT AND APPROVAL

6 ASSESSING SUCCESS

Meetings would be easy to control if we only invited people who are easy to handle. No one likes the sort of meetings where the chairperson is ruling with a rod of iron and everyone is afraid to open their mouths. On the other hand, no one likes the meetings that run themselves, because a totally ineffectual chairperson dithers about, afraid of upsetting anyone by controlling behaviour and these meetings get more and more unpleasant.

So how do we get the balance right? Running a good agenda, and inviting the right people and not the wrong ones will help, but more to the point, by controlling the meeting effectively.

By chairing a meeting well, people will have a chance to say whatever is relevant, but not be allowed to dominate discussion unnecessarily. People who are quiet will be drawn out, so their opinions are heard too. Everyone will feel they have participated and been heard.

IS THIS YOU?

■ A chairperson should run the meeting and everyone else should listen and speak when invited. It's the only way to keep control.

■ I don't like all this talk — it sounds like manipulating people. I'm not Machiavelli!

■ I'm not a chairperson really — I call the meetings, but I just do the work — no-one's really in charge . . .

■ Our meetings are OK. But it's really hard to get some people to join in — like getting blood out of a stone.

■ I cope fairly well. I mean, no one complains and they all come back next time.

1 · PLANNING AND PREPARATION

Remember the formula for a successful meeting given in Chapter 1? Now we can add some more detail, so as chairperson of a meeting you understand the aspects of your role and how to progress the meeting successfully.

AGENDA +	PARTICIPANTS =	RESULTS
■ Realistic	■ Introductions	■ Satisfaction
■ Purposeful (to inform, consult or decide)	■ Motivation	■ Achievement of business
■ Structured	■ Listening	
	■ Control	
	■ Summary	

The agenda

In the last chapter we looked at the agenda but your planning doesn't stop there. You also need to do your homework.

- Has an item arisen before?
- If so, what happened then?
- Who supported it and opposed it?
- Have they changed their view?
- What is the likely result this time?
- Your fallback position – what you will try to achieve if the item itself is unsuccessful.

Participants

Now that (hopefully) you have the right people at the meeting, it still isn't plain sailing. You need to ensure they participate. People skills, communication skills, and interpersonal skills – call it what you will, leading and facilitating a discussion is whole enormous subject. Here, let's just focus on a few behaviours that will help: introductions, motivation, listening, control and summary. You can prepare introductions and at least do some work to prepare summaries.

Motivation is not just motivating people at the meeting, it also involves preparation. Finding out what people's motivation is beforehand can explain why they behave in a certain way when a certain issue is raised. Listening and control really have to be done at the meeting.

Results

Results are not just achieving the business. You also need for people to *feel* they have achieved at the end of the meeting. Otherwise, they will be tempted to raise the same issues again and again — because although they were resolved, people *feel* they weren't resolved.

> *'You don't just have to achieve what you need to in a meeting, you have to be seen to have achieved it by the participants.'*

2 · INTRODUCTIONS

People introductions

Introductions can be useful at a meeting. Sometimes, you may think everyone knows each other, but in today's world, it is common for people to know each other only by telephone and email. It's useful to just check whether everyone recognises all the faces round the table.

Purpose introductions

Once names and a quick 'who's who' has been established, it is sometimes useful to say *why* people are present. You can do this yourself as chairperson, or invite each person to state this (although this can be dangerous if they don't know or think they're there for another reason entirely). It's often useful to say something like: 'George is here to talk about sales figures, and I'm hoping he'll also help us with facts on marketing ideas later. Teresa I know is particularly interested in the canteen issues, so although she doesn't usually attend, I thought including her made sense.'

These types of statement give everyone a clear idea of why they're there, and can give confidence to someone who is usually reticent or shy about speaking up.

Agenda introductions

Then it is useful to quickly introduce the agenda. Check everyone has it, and if not, don't give out spare copies – it encourages them to believe that not bringing it and preparing is acceptable at your meetings. They can share if they have forgotten it. Of course, keep a couple of secret copies so that if someone is without the agenda because they didn't get one, *they* can have a spare copy.

It may seem as if these three introductions are going to take up the first 20 minutes of what may only be a short meeting. Obviously, you don't need to do any of these if it isn't appropriate, but sometimes it is. In any event, each can be covered in a sentence or two, and all three can be accomplished in a couple of minutes. For more formal meetings, you may even want to make introductions the first item on the agenda.

Item introductions

Each item on the agenda should have a quick introduction. You must have been to many meetings where it went something like: 'Item 2, staff suggestions – Caroline?' and poor Caroline was left to do the item herself. As your agenda should have a purpose, remind people of it. 'Item 2 – staff suggestions. Caroline's going to run through them so we can decide which is worth considering fully at the next meeting.'

> *'Introductions can pave the way for success by pointing participants in the right direction, like a sheepdog gently nudging sheep towards the required goal.'*

3 · DISCUSSION AND PARTICIPATION

Group size and participation

The larger the group, the harder it is to control participation. Also, people may have questions or comments that are relevant and valuable – but not to the whole meeting. They either raise these, and you risk losing half the meeting's attention, or they don't raise them and you miss valuable points. Keep the number of participants low enough that they feel free and encouraged to participate.

Consider breaks

We have mentioned before that breaks stop attention spans from being exceeded. They can also encourage participation. Sometimes an informal five minutes at the start of a meeting to get tea or coffee can break the ice, and produce discussion and participation that might otherwise not occur. Similarly, a break for refreshments during a meeting can produce some useful debate and discussion, or put a stop to some unwanted excessive participation. Use breaks wisely.

Motivation

■ Bring in quiet people – don't let them sit there in silence – or you'll never know what they might have contributed.

■ To encourage input from a quiet person, you may have to put them on the spot to motivate them to speak up. With others, gentle questioning or asking opinions may work.

■ Be open about needing input from the group because of your own lack of knowledge. This motivates people by making them feel important.

■ To stimulate a debate or discussion, call on opposing viewpoints alternately. This motivates by letting people know you aren't biased but balanced, and will listen to everyone.

■ Occasionally, where the problem is shutting people up rather than not getting them to speak, it may be better to assign, say, ten minutes to debate on one side, then ten minutes for the opposing views. This prevents discussion running on, getting adversarial or out of hand.

Listening

■ Listening is not passive, it's active. Use nods, looks, eye contact, questions, etc. to show people you are listening. It can be a good example to others.

■ A useful ploy to stop interruptions is to deal with the

interrupter not by stopping them interrupting, which is challenging them, but to ask them the favour of letting you listen. Try something like 'Do you mind waiting, Gemma – I need to listen carefully to this as I'm not an expert in this area.'

- No matter what your own opinion is, as chairperson you should always try to see the other person's point of view whilst you are listening to them.

- Listen to the minority, and if necessary, speak for them if you are the only one who heard them, by repeating their view.

Controlling

- Remember at all times that above all else, people attending a meeting will expect the chairperson to do something to control that meeting.

- You can control by choosing and using allies and enemies, rather than by directly making your own views known.

- There are many methods of direct control – formal procedures, timing, and behaviour. A well-written agenda is a means of control.

- Control discussions and contributions above all else. Too light or too heavy a hand must be avoided as you are attempting to control people who want to voice their opinions and feelings.

- Control through courtesy is always very effective.

- Never let multiple meetings or side discussions start.

- Always know when to give in, to preserve 'the integrity of the chair'. There is no legal substance to the concept of a 'casting vote' but people are so used to the idea that many people fear chairpersons will be biased. Chairing a meeting doesn't mean you have be neutral, but you do have to be seen to be fair and just, which is what is meant by 'the integrity of the chair' – not abusing your status to get your own way.

> *'Participation can be encouraged or discouraged by a good chairperson. A degree of participation is essential if people are to truly support and implement the matters discussed, and not change their minds later.'*

4 · HANDLING CONFLICT

When conflict arises, it is often more than just unpleasant – it's counter-productive. People arguing conflicting views may even make out of character or illogical decisions, so to keep meetings on track it's important to be able to handle conflict effectively.

Facts vs opinions

Many confrontations arise because of a conflict between facts and opinions. Let's look at the difference.

Facts	Opinions
Known to be true	Believed to be true
Can be proved	Can only be justified or supported
Based on research, knowledge or experience	Based on preconceived ideas and/or beliefs

Laid out like this, it's easy to tell the difference. But in the heat of a meeting, even one without conflict, getting to the bottom of whether an idea or input is based on fact or opinion can be tricky.

■ People tend to argue positions with opinions rather than facts.

■ People state opinions as facts – but without proof it is still an opinion.

To handle conflict, try to prevent people from expressing opinions and restrict discussion to facts. Challenge opinions that are represented as facts but that obviously have no proof to substantiate them. Consider listing all the facts and then all the opinions, and discussing and making decisions giving less weight to the opinions.

Disagreement vs argument

Disagreement is part of discussion – you can't expect everyone to agree all the time – it's unrealistic. Disagreements force people to think and make decisions based on varying points of view, which is a good thing. Argument, on the other hand, is something else. Argument usually has an emotional element and may arise because:

■ Someone will be emotionally affected by the outcome.

- Someone has an emotional attachment to the issue/project/ item.

- Personal history is brought into the issue, which again involves emotional attachment.

- Always try to restrict argument if at all possible. It is hard to stop once it gets going because emotions are running wild. Because of the emotions involved, you may well find it is based on opinion not fact, which may help you stop it at the outset.

Managing conflict when it breaks out

- Deal with it – the sooner the better. Things are harder to stop once momentum is reached.

- Stop side discussions and make people all pay attention to and participate in the one discussion.

- Be open and honest. Say, 'The meeting has started to deteriorate.' Just pointing it out can sometimes relieve pressure.

- Ask for help. For example, 'Can we please all calm down and discuss the issue sensibly.'

- Try not to threaten: Never say things like, 'If things don't simmer down I'll have to stop the meeting and start again when things have calmed down a little.' There's nothing wrong with *doing* that, but *threatening* to do it is often something that only adds fuel to the flame.

- Find something people can agree on – establish common ground. Outline points of agreement.

- Prevent interruptions. Force people to wait until someone has finished before questioning or responding.

> *'Chairing meetings is extraordinarily difficult, but the skills required can be planned and learned over time.'*

5 · GAINING AGREEMENT AND APPROVAL

Gaining approval or agreement is sometimes difficult. There are many ways to achieve this.

- Bring discussion to an end.

- Let people know it is time to make a decision or to agree something.

- Summarise different viewpoints.

- Discourage interruptions.

- Ask for a decision or viewpoint.

- Make sure the minority or quiet people speak up, even if you have to ask them to.

- If several people want to speak, you can go 'round the table' in turn, but keep comments short.

- Summarise opinion.

- Take a vote if necessary. This can be dangerous if it goes against you. Sometimes it is better not to vote unless you have to tip the balance. This is not a casting vote (which is where the side the chairperson votes with wins in the event of a tie) but just a single vote the same as everyone else.

Golden rules

■ Agree or decide.

■ Confirm what you have agreed or decided.

■ Specify
  – what will be done
  – who will do it
  – by when.

■ Record the decision in the notes or minutes.

> *'Getting agreement is easy. Getting everyone to agree afterwards about exactly what was agreed is the hard part!'*

6 · ASSESSING SUCCESS

Closing the meeting

At the end of the meeting, the chairperson should give a quick summary. Sometimes, although rarely seen, it can help to just run through the agenda and state what was agreed or decided. Action to be taken away and done can also be pointed out again. This leaves everyone in no doubt about what they need to do.

Satisfaction and achievement of business

At the beginning of this chapter, we saw the formula for a successful meeting. Under 'results', we listed achievement of business and satisfaction. Ideally, we would like both.

You can't always guarantee you'll achieve the business, but if people leave the meeting with a sense of satisfaction and achievement, at least the meeting will not have been in vain. On the other hand, beware of achieving the business at the expense of people's satisfaction.

A story...

A friend of mine used to tell a story about a school governors' meeting. Typically these meetings went on all evening until late at night, and involved endless debate. One day, the chairman was unable to attend, and asked my friend to chair the meeting. He chaired it with great efficiency, preventing unconstructive debate and discussion, and the meeting finished in a little under two hours. He felt a great sense of achievement.

He was just going to his car to drive home when he overheard some of the participants talking in the car park. In short, they thought the meeting was awful – rushed, unpleasant, with none of the usual friendly, interested atmosphere. Further-more, they had decided not to attend if he chaired the meeting again.

This is a prime example of achieving the business of the meeting, but at the expense of people's satisfaction. Some of the governors were elderly, most were retired, and their monthly meeting had become something of a social event, and a major source of their personal sense of achievement and importance in the community. Rightly or wrongly, part of their purpose in attending the meeting was because they enjoyed it. They didn't feel the meeting had been at all successful, even though all the items had been covered. So the meeting didn't really achieve all its purpose, did it? It might even waste more time in the long run, as people may well raise the same points again, as they don't feel they were covered 'properly' at this meeting.

Compromises

Of course, it would be ludicrous to let that meeting continue unchecked, using up people's time in endless debate. It's a waste of time and money, but with a little thought, there *are* alternatives. A compromise would achieve both results – completion of business – as well as satisfying the participants. Here are some ideas:

■ Get the meeting over quickly, but give some tasks to a **sub-committee** or **working group** to continue with. They can then debate points which they feel strongly about outside the meeting, and bring the results to the next meeting.

■ Speak to people. Explain you have a set time limit for the formal meeting, then people who wish to can leave. After this time, discussion can be raised on any subject, and you can either chair this discussion or appoint someone else so you can leave.

■ Establish pre-meetings. This is where small groups of people get together to discuss one particular issue, and then run through their findings at the main meeting. It's like a working group, but immediately before the meeting. These are very useful, as you can have your own pre-meeting as well to brief key people on anticipated problems, or to quietly deal with anyone disruptive before the meeting. They can also be divisive, however, as people not invited may feel left out.

> *'Meetings need to satisfy the participants as well as the agenda.'*

IN SUMMARY

■ Preparation is the key to running meetings.

■ Short introductions make the path to success a lot easier.

■ Encourage discussion and participation — people feel more committed if they are involved in making decisions.

■ Chairing meetings must be balanced. Above all, people expect you to control with integrity.

■ Make sure you guide people to making a decision or coming to an agreement, and ensure everyone knows what exactly has been agreed.

■ Remember that not only does the meeting need to achieve business, but also people have to be satisfied that this has been done. Pre-meetings can help.

5 · Participating in Other People's Meetings

You don't just have to work at meetings when you're running them. There's a lot you can do to help control your destiny at other people's meetings.

In this Chapter:

Meetings that we attend as participants can be doubly frustrating as we aren't in control. Poor or aggressive chairing can make anyone feel negative. It is important to know how to guide a meeting and exert influence over events without being the chairperson.

As a last resort, you could always take over yourself. But that doesn't make you feel or look good; it rarely does anything but harm the chairperson; and often makes other participants feel upset too.

More subtle methods of steering the meeting are better. Good communication helps, as well as preparation. If you deal with others effectively, the meeting is much more likely to stay on track and get somewhere.

Meetings we participate in can also be committees/working parties. These report to a main meeting, and often don't have formal leadership. The lack of control can be an issue, so your behaviour can be even more important at these than at chaired meetings.

IS THIS YOU?

- I hate meetings where I'm not in control.
- It doesn't matter what I think. He has the casting vote, doesn't he?
- I wish George would get a grip. He lets everyone ramble on all day.
- Meetings are just talking to people. I don't need to read about how to do that.

1 · GOOD COMMUNICATION

There are many good books on communication. In the HowTo series, *Managing Yourself* deals with assertive behaviour and communication. Here are five main communication techniques that will assist you at even the most difficult meetings.

Acknowledgement/recognition

Acknowledgement/recognition is about making people feel good – acknowledging and recognising them and their contribution; making them feel you value them and their opinion. If people know you want to listen to them, they don't have to shout and interrupt to be heard. Here are some examples of recognition/acknowledgement behaviour during a meeting. (Note that there are examples of using them in response to negative as well as positive behaviour.)

- I'm glad to see you here, as you know a lot more than I do about this.

- We really need your expertise on this one.

- That isn't really what I was looking for, but it's a good example of the sort of information and level of detail we're looking for.

- Thanks for that – you obviously put some effort into gathering this information for us.

- I think there's something in that we can build on.

- That's great. Can you make a note of that for me?

- I know it didn't work out last time you tried it, but I'm sure you can handle it now we've been through it once.

- Thank you. These meetings aren't always pleasant, but I like the way you handle them.

■ That would have been a lot more difficult without you there.

Disclosure

Disclosure is when you give people some information about yourself, to encourage them to do the same. People do it in order to make others feel close enough to be comfortable 'opening up'. It's about giving information away, so just be careful you don't give too much away.

■ I think the most important thing is . . .

■ I'm glad we met here because . . .

■ I'm concerned we don't have all the facts yet.

■ This decision makes me uncomfortable. We tried it before and it wasn't really that successful. Can we check all our options first?

■ I admit I had my doubts, but now I'm sold on the idea – I think it's great.

■ I know we can do this if we just take a little more time to think.

■ We should do this more often.

■ I hope this doesn't turn out too badly – I must say I don't feel totally confident.

■ Involvement

Involvement is about getting people involved in the meeting. It's about encouraging participation.

- Can we all stay on this topic? Jumping about distracts me.
- What questions do you have?
- How does this affect you and your team?
- Would you like to add anything?
- Do you have any ideas?
- Could you follow up on that, as you thought of it?
- Can we just recap quickly, so I know exactly where we are?
- When do you think we could get a result on this?

Empathy

Empathy is showing you understand the way someone feels. It's about how they feel, and not about what they are saying or doing.

- I know it's disappointing to come back to the table on this when we thought this had all been resolved but . . .

■ You're right to feel pleased with yourselves – we've made good progress so far.

■ I can sense your frustration, but we do need to make a decision although it's not important to all of us.

■ It's obvious this is an emotive issue for you. Personal feelings are important, but we shouldn't decide on that basis.

■ I know you feel pressurised; but time's getting on and we need to get through this.

■ I get the feeling you're uncomfortable or even unhappy with that. Would you like to tell us what your reservations are?

■ It must be a relief to have got to the bottom of this.

■ I share your anxiety, but we can't do anything here and now.

Support

Support is when you express support for someone else.

■ I'm happy to chair the debate, but the decision needs to belong to all of us.

■ I think that as John's in charge, he should start.

- I can give my opinion, but Michelle has all the real facts on this.

- Of course I'm happy to let you have more information, but I'd like to hear from you first so I know exactly what you need.

- I've got some ideas, but you know best — it's your team this affects.

- Don't give up — let's run through it once more.

- How can I help you get this ready in time?

- If anyone needs help on this, let me know, will you?

'Good communication is a huge subject, but just a few techniques can work wonders.'

2 · HANDLING CHALLENGES

Challenges or opposition are hard to handle, especially when you aren't the one controlling the meeting. If the chairperson doesn't deal with them, you need to do it yourself.

Implications of challenges and confrontation

- Time is wasted.
- The agenda is halted until disagreements are resolved.
- The meeting doesn't get its results.
- More meetings may be necessary.
- Morale declines.
- Relationships may be damaged or even broken.
- People lose trust and confidence in you and others.
- People become frustrated.
- People avoid future meetings.

Focus on issues

The problem is that to most people, winning or losing to someone else is the main thing in a meeting, not the issue itself. Focus on the issue, not the behaviour or opinion of others by sticking to logic and facts. You can try to 'win arguments' by summarising the other person's point of view, gaining their agreement, then explaining why it won't work – this is logic/fact at work. But if all they are interested in is their feelings and opinions they may not even care about facts – we've all seen completely illogical decisions.

Enlist support

You can try to bring in others on your side. This can help, but can also turn the whole meeting into a disagreement between two opposing sides, like an unruly football match. In these situations, it sometimes helps to remember you are all aiming at the same goal, not at two different ends of the pitch, and remind others of that fact.

Take time out

Suggest a break. During this time, you and your opponent(s) can both have a think about how to proceed, or even get together and try to resolve things in privacy. You can even suggest the matter is postponed until the next meeting, to give a chance for things to cool down and become less confrontational.

Keep control

Never lose your temper. Back off before others lose theirs.

Give in

Sometimes it is better to give in gracefully, and then raise the matter with a higher authority, or again at another time. This can be frustrating, but often works.

Tips for handling and preventing challenge

- Speak confidently.

- Stop people from interrupting or asking you questions until you're finished – politely: 'Sorry, George, can I finish and then answer you?'

- Never use weak phrases such as 'I'm not sure if...', or 'I don't know whether...' Replace with positive language such as 'I think...' or 'It seems to me...'

- Don't phrase your points as a question – often done by raising your tone of voice at the end of a sentence....?

- Remember body language, and don't fidget or fiddle when you are speaking. Confident eye contact can give the 'Don't mess with me' message very politely.

> *'Don't let meetings get opposing if possible. But if it can't be avoided, deal with it effectively.'*

3 · THE UNEXPECTED TOPIC

Sometimes we are in a meeting and suddenly find topics being discussed for which we aren't prepared. This is easy to handle if it's your meeting, but if you are trapped in somebody else's, it can be hard to avoid ending up 'on the spot'.

Deal with things quickly

- As soon as you believe things are going away from the expected, say something: 'Sorry, but I think I may have misunderstood this item. I thought...'

- If you can proceed with a little backup, additional information or support, ask if people mind you getting it. Phone for information or to check with somebody about what you should say.

- If you are completely unprepared and really can't discuss things, explain so clearly and politely, and ask if the meeting can be rescheduled.

- Never blame anyone else — be graceful. Never say anything like: 'I can't help it if the agenda wasn't clear'.

■ If you are 'caught on the hop' and have to participate when you are unprepared, don't be afraid to reply again later when you have had a chance to check the information. Send an email or note to all participants: 'As a follow-up to the meeting, I need to clarify the following.'

> **'Don't panic when confronted with unexpected topics. Just tread carefully.'**

4 · DEALING WITH INEFFECTIVE CONTROL

When a chairperson isn't in control of a meeting, the meeting and all the participants can suffer. There are ways to deal with this, depending on the meeting and how you feel.

Volunteer

Volunteer to lead the discussion. This is taking over the meeting, but if you say 'shall I lead this discussion?' or some other phrase, it gives the chairperson a get-out without losing face.

Take notes or minutes

This is often seen as a junior role, or secretarial issue, but it can be very powerful. It gives you an excuse to interrupt and slow things down, to hear from everyone under the guise of wanting to get all the facts down correctly. In fact, it can give you an opportunity to stealthily take over chairing the meeting without people being aware of it.

Set a good example

Ask permission to contribute, ask the chairperson what's next, etc. Lead people into looking to the chairperson for guidance and control, and others may follow your example. Discourage others from *not* regarding the chairperson seriously: 'Hang on Jane, Greg's in charge. Let's see what he wants to do first.'

Launch an attack

If the situation is extreme and really warrants it, you can suggest to the meeting that you take over and ask for support. It's a very drastic step, and one of the main reasons is that if you do it, others may decide *they* can do it to *you*.

> **'Ineffective control is frustrating, but you can do a great deal without taking over and publicly deposing the chairperson.'**

5 · TIPS FOR SITTING IT OUT

Sometimes, you are trapped in a boring or unproductive meeting. Maybe you need to wait for a later agenda item that involves you. Maybe you just aren't in a position to avoid being there. There are ways to deal with this.

Excusing yourself politely

- The bigger the meeting, the harder it can be to find the confidence to leave.

- Wait for a gap in the conversation before politely excusing yourself.

■ Make a polite explanation. Needing to get back to work *is* a valid reason, although it may not make you popular.

If you don't want to excuse yourself

Maybe the meeting is being held by someone important, or you are required to attend. Either way, you need some strategies for passing the time.

■ Use a notebook or paper and try to do some work.

■ Always keep looking up from time to time so it appears you are note-taking.

■ Nod and make encouraging 'listening signals' occasionally.

■ Find something to occupy your mind so that you don't get sleepy. Dozing off in meetings can cause real offence and create a bad image of you with others.

Never:

■ Try to liven things up by making comments or jokes that aren't relevant.

- Use impatient body language – tapping pens, shuffling feet, crossing and uncrossing legs, looking at the clock or door every few minutes.

- Don't stare at the person speaking. It can make you become even more sleepy, and will put you first in line for being asked any questions.

> **'Either excuse yourself gracefully, or wait it out in style.'**

6 · ESTABLISHING COMMITTEES AND WORKING PARTIES

There are many reasons for establishing committees or working parties. Mainly, they take an issue or range of issues outside the main meeting. Typically, local authorities work in this way, with committees for education, social services, highways, etc., all being separate, and the leaders of each of those committees presenting results to the main council meeting.

It's a very effective way of working, as it can be very useful for limiting the time the main meeting takes. Here are some advantages and disadvantages before you decide these are an excellent idea, as they are not without risk.

Advantages of committees/working parties

- You can get more done with fewer people present.
- You can focus on one issue or range of issues.
- They can be less formal, and bring people together.
- They can be less threatening for quiet people to put their point of view.
- You can bring in experts or people with information/skills that aren't part of the main meeting.
- You can test people's opinions outside the main meeting.
- You can iron out problems in greater privacy.
- You can strike deals with people.
- It saves time during the main meeting.

Disadvantages of committees/working parties

■ The meeting may resent or not accept your decision/input.

■ You can be lulled into a false sense of security, and then meet stronger opposition in the main meeting.

■ People can become alienated, because they aren't part of the committee/working party.

■ It can cause the members a lot more work, because they basically have two meetings (unless they have only one or two representatives that report back to the main meeting).

■ They can get bogged down in detail or technicalities of the issue.

■ They can be easier to dominate unless someone takes charge.

'Splitting away contentious or technical issues can make meetings an awful lot more manageable.'

IN SUMMARY

■ Build on five behaviours in communicating with others: recognition, disclosure, involvement, empathy and support.

■ Never lose your temper. Focus on issues, not behaviour.

■ Deal with unexpected topics without getting totally flustered. You can always address issues later if necessary.

■ Take steps in meetings where the chairperson is not in control. Support them, or in an emergency, take over either overtly or covertly as necessary.

■ Learn to excuse yourself gracefully where necessary, or even wait out the meeting without creating a bad impression.

■ Committees and/or working parties can assist the main meeting by taking issues outside the meeting itself and reporting back.

6 · Getting Results and Action

'Agreeing what is to be done is a skill – we often think we've done it, only to find out we actually haven't...'

In this Chapter:

1 CREATIVE THINKING

---

2 VOTING

---

3 WRITING MINUTES

---

4 ENCOURAGING FOLLOW-UP

---

5 AFTER THE MEETING

The problem with getting action is getting the **precise** action agreed on. It can be surprisingly difficult getting the right people to do exactly what was agreed, by the time it was agreed.

People very often agree things at a meeting and then have a change of heart, or decisions made mean subtly different things to different people. People even forget (or pretend they don't remember) agreeing to something. Minutes are critical for achieving the agreed results.

Minutes are also useful for getting people to do tasks allocated to them during a meeting. Good minutes not only give a record of the meeting, they also give a list of allocated tasks, for review at the next meeting.

Finally, after a meeting you don't just go away and forget about it until next time. There's still work you can do to improve chances of success next time around.

IS THIS YOU?

- If I suggested we vote, they'd laugh at me. We don't bother with all that nonsense.

■ No one reads the minutes anyway, so I don't take much effort to produce them any more.

■ You have to trust people. I just let them get on with it, you can't keep checking up on people.

■ It takes more time to write the wretched minutes up and send them out than it does to hold the meeting.

1 · CREATIVE THINKING

When considering a problem or trying to resolve an issue, you need to generate ideas and potential solutions. The most common way to stimulate creative thinking is **brainstorming**. Brainstorming isn't just something we use to describe sitting and thinking of as many ideas as possible – it's a definite process which was invented in the 1940s by an American advertising executive called Osborn.

Using brainstorming in meetings

There are many books and sources of information on brainstorming, but what is more useful in this context is how to apply brainstorming techniques successfully in a meeting.

Before the meeting – preparation for brainstorming

■ When you schedule the meeting, give participants a brief outline of the problem and its history. This helps people to prepare and focus.

■ If you want people to prepare, tell them so and explain why.

■ Consider inviting one or two people with different backgrounds and perspectives – a fresh view point can assist.

■ Having said that, be careful over who else you invite – senior people or strangers may make people more reluctant to participate freely themselves. Use your own judgement.

Set rules and let people know them

Inform people of the brainstorming guidelines. This gives them rules, so they feel safe participating freely, and reduces any anxiety that their ideas will be ridiculed or discounted.

■ No criticism of ideas is allowed.

■ All ideas are good and are to be encouraged, no matter how wild or unlikely.

■ The more ideas the better.

■ Everyone should try to build on or combine the ideas of others.

Run the session effectively

■ Don't let sessions run on for more than about 40 minutes – if you haven't got a useful solution or idea by then, let people know you'll reconvene, and if possible arrange a time and date then and there, so they can continue to think about it in the meantime.

■ Explain at the beginning that negative feedback, negative behaviour, criticism or laughing at ideas etc. will not be tolerated.

■ Warn people that you expect supportive behaviour towards everyone and their ideas.

■ Ask people to build on other people's ideas where possible.

■ Consider breaking the participants into subgroups and have each team brainstorm separately as a competition, or have each of them work on a different aspect of the problem or issue. The smaller the group, the more likely people are to feel comfortable and at ease, so they are more likely to contribute freely.

■ Put the objective, problem or issue up on a wall or flipchart where everyone can see it. This will keep subconsciously reminding them of the issue at hand. The very best thing is to phrase it as a question.

■ Capture all ideas where people can see them. Don't record them in a notebook – the important thing is that the sight of ideas will stimulate new ones, or building on them. So use a flipchart or whiteboard, so all the ideas are visible to everyone at all times.

■ Help people if things start to flag and ideas dry up. Step in before they have dried up. Try reading out ideas, or asking people to pick their favourite and say why – discuss the existing ideas – anything to keep conversation going, which will make new ideas pop into people's minds.

- Don't share your own ideas all at once. Jot them down and keep them up your sleeve for when things start to slow down, and then add them to restart the flow of ideas.

After the session

- If you have had a solution identified within the group, great. Remind people in writing what was decided and who was responsible – it never hurts to give people recognition.

- If not, arrange the ideas in groups and send them out. Ask people to look at them, and to suggest the best answer or a compromise between ideas.

- Whatever you do thank everyone for their ideas.

'Brainstorming is excellent for generating ideas, and a group can always come up with more ideas than one individual.'

2 · VOTING

Some meetings are more formal than others, and include a formal voting structure. Meetings that are informal often don't even take votes.

The 'casting vote'

This is where, in the event of a tie, the vote is decided by the vote of the chairperson. It's equivalent to the chairperson having two votes, in fact. Remember, there is no legal basis for a 'casting vote', however, you may wish to use it. For example, if there is an even number of people at your meeting, a tie is possible. How will you resolve this? Giving someone (the chairperson, an expert, the person most affected by the decision) a casting vote can prevent a tie.

Secret balloting

Secret votes can be made on slips of paper (like an election) or people can use a counter of some kind – for example a penny, and ask them to put it in a box for or against. This can avoid embarrassment if someone wishes to vote without others knowing, if some people are underconfident, or if one person is intimidating. However, it is hardly a technique for fostering team spirit and good communication, and doesn't address the issues of why people are afraid to vote openly. Sometimes it can be useful, but it is rarely recommended.

Other voting methods

The most common method is probably a show of hands, asking people to raise their hand depending on which decision they support. This is rarely used for small and/or informal meetings. A better option is to go round the table, and ask everyone for a decision and a short explanation about their decision. Then before deciding, give people a chance to change their mind. This is extremely important, as someone's reason for voting a certain way may have changed someone else's mind.

Consider whether voting is an appropriate way to resolve an issue.

■ Do you need a decision?

- Do you need agreement or can one person make the decision?

- Are there an odd number of voters?

- Should the chairperson take part in a vote?

- Do you want the chairperson or someone else to have the casting vote?

- Should the vote be public or private?

'Sometimes a vote is necessary, but you should think carefully about how you organise this.'

3 · WRITING MINUTES

Minutes are notes of the meeting. There are many different formats, depending on how formal the meetings are. But any minutes or meeting notes should contain several common items:

- The date and time of the meeting.
- Who was present.
- Decisions made.
- Actions agreed.
- Who will carry out the actions.
- Action deadline.
- Date and time of the next meeting.
- How to submit agenda items.

It is common to lay the minutes out in columns, with the item number on the left, then the agenda item, then the discussion, and a column on the right for the name or initials of anyone needing to take action. You may prefer to send out a separate 'action list' after a meeting to everyone who was tasked with any action, listing what he or she are to do and by when. This is in addition to the minutes.

You might also like to have two lists at the start of the minutes: people present and people absent. It's surprising how most meetings list people present and those who apologised for not being there. People who just didn't turn up are omitted completely, which doesn't tell them this was inconsiderate and to be discouraged. Give the message that attending is noted, apologies are accepted but not mentioned, and people inexplicably absent are listed for all to see. The first time you do this at a meeting you may get a lot of irate phone calls, but very few or no non-attendees next time – unless they have explained themselves.

Minutes made by others:

- Check these carefully.

- Speak up as soon as you notice there is an error or discrepancy.

- Voice your concerns politely and avoid blaming anyone:
  'My recollection is that...',
  not 'You seem to have noted incorrectly...'

- Point out the change you would like to see clearly, with suggestion not direction:
  'Item 4 should reflect that the meeting decided to...'
  not 'You need to amend item 4 to reflect this'.

'Minutes need not be complicated, so long as you always include the basics.'

4 · ENCOURAGING FOLLOW-UP

■ Assign tasks as they arise. As soon as an item needs action, ask the appropriate person to follow up, and if nobody in particular needs to do it, ask for a volunteer. Allocating tasks as you go along like this stops one person picking up everything and others getting off too lightly, as it's apparent as you go along who is picking up most of the workload.

■ If nobody volunteers, ask again, and point out that if there are no volunteers you will need to allocate the job.

■ Whoever is taking notes or minutes needs to note the item, the action required, who is responsible and the deadline.

■ Get people to agree deadlines – don't make summations or enforce them on people.

■ Review the action list before leaving the meeting, at the end.

- Send out a quick summary email to confirm in writing who is expected to do what and by when.

- At the beginning of the next meeting, go through the action list before doing anything else. This gets people used to the idea that they really are expected to do what they are tasked with each time.

'Make it easy for people to take action after the meeting by being clear and reminding them appropriately.'

5 · AFTER THE MEETING

After the meeting, there is still work to do.

- Review your performance, and ask yourself 'how could I do that differently? What would have changed if I had?'

- Ask yourself what you have learned about the other people that will help you in future meetings with them.

- Did you achieve what you wanted? If not, why not?

- Have a word with anyone who left the meeting with negative feelings, to try to repair any damage done to relationships.

- Also have a word with anyone behaving badly, to try to prevent occurrences in future.

- Ask yourself whether this is a meeting you should stop going to. Was it a waste of your time?

- Circulate notes or minutes.

- Brief people who couldn't attend if necessary in addition to the minutes.

- Take any necessary action.

- Start planning the next meeting.

> *'Just as there is necessary preparation before a meeting, you need to take some action afterwards.'*

IN SUMMARY

■ Encourage creative thinking to resolve difficult problems.

■ Think carefully about voting, and ensure you use the right method.

■ Produce a record of decisions taken and tasks allocated for action, even if you don't write formal minutes.

■ Ensure people follow up by actually doing what was agreed.

■ Don't just 'switch off' after a meeting. Analyse it and what went well and badly. Think about why, and learn from experience.

7 · The Latest Technology and Meetings

With new technology, your meetings can be more efficient and effective, or an even worse disaster!

In this Chapter:

1 SIMPLE TECHNOLOGY
SOLUTIONS

2 TELECONFERENCING

3 VIDEOCONFERENCING

4 INTERNET OR WEB
CONFERENCING

Meetings are changing. New technology is changing the way we work, and meetings are no exception. But it can be very daunting being invited to a videoconference, or asked to do a web presentation.

This chapter looks at the new technology and how it can be used in meetings. It gives you hints and tips on handling the various technologies to make meetings as productive and effective as possible.

The new technology won't necessarily make meetings more difficult – it can often make life easier, once you get used to it, and are aware of what's involved.

1 · SIMPLE TECHNOLOGY SOLUTIONS

New technology should help make meetings more effective, otherwise why bother using it? Let's look at electronic meetings in general before we examine the details of the various options available.

Cost reduction

Meetings which do not require people to travel can save a great deal of money. Although it can be expensive to set up a videoconference, for example, this is almost always far cheaper than having people travel in person back and forth to a meeting, especially when you consider their time as well as the direct expenses.

Conferencing technology

Conferencing technology – whatever form you use, means people can stay in their usual location and still 'attend' a meeting. Initiatives such as Microsoft Net Meeting enable meeting participants to share documents and applications.

Virtual meeting spaces are available to avoid the problems often associated with corporate IT systems – firewalls etc. Virtual meeting spaces are places where anyone with a web browser can hold an online meeting with password protection. In these meetings you can usually share applications, documents and sometimes audio.

Simple tips to use technology for effective meetings

- Schedule meetings electronically if possible – eg on Outlook or Lotus notes, or any other shared diary system. Using this to check availability saves time ringing round to find out people's availability (which can be a lengthy process).

■ Use a laptop to take minutes or notes – may be distracting, but saves writing them up later, if people are happy for you to do this.

■ Avoid meeting at all if things can be resolved by a simple (maybe even three-way) phone call.

■ Show presentations on PowerPoint or similar, rather than bor-ing paper notes for people to follow. It keeps people's atten-tion, and can be faster to amend with any feedback. For example, when reviewing something, have it on screen and make amendments then and there as people agree them.

> *'Technology doesn't have to be complicated – use it where you can to make life a little easier.'*

2 · TELECONFERENCING

Teleconferencing needn't be daunting. Follow these simple rules for good teleconferences.

Before the call

- Plan ahead in good time – it's hard, and may cost a fee to change teleconferences.

- Send out any printed or email material in advance – agenda, papers, background information etc.

- Emphasise the importance of calling in on time – it can waste a great deal of people's time if they are waiting for people to dial in to the meeting/call.

During the call

- Check who is present by checking names. Summarise periodically, so people know who is now present.

- If people don't know each other, take time for a brief introduction – it can be hard talking to faceless strangers.

- Try not to wait for latecomers unless this is absolutely necessary. Move on, and when they do call in, make them wait for a gap in the conversation before recapping for them.

- Run through any ground rules – for example, it may be helpful if people always identify themselves by name before speaking.

■ Remember, communication is hard with no visual content.

■ Try to avoid throwing questions or discussions out to the group as a whole – always direct them at individuals in turn. Otherwise, people may all talk at once, and make it impossible to hear properly. It may even blank out the sound temporarily.

■ Check periodically that people haven't been 'lost', by directing a question or comment to them – just check they are still there.

The pitfalls

Communication experts tell us that when we communicate:

■ 10 per cent of the meaning is contained in the words we choose

■ 20 per cent is contained in the style of delivery

■ 70 per cent is contained in non-verbal cues or body language.

This quickly explains why teleconferencing is not very effective communication, doesn't it? With only 30 per cent of information coming in, communication is hard work.

> *'Teleconferences are the simplest form of technological meeting, and handled sensibly are not too difficult.*

3 · VIDEOCONFERENCING

Most people really don't like videoconferencing. However, the use of videoconferences is still growing, and technology to carry them out is reducing in cost all the time.

Location

■ Avoid windows or corridors where people can be seen walking past the room on the monitor. It's distracting.

■ Keep videoconferences away from noisy areas which can disrupt sound.

■ Minimise interruptions. In a recent video interview, I was amazed to see a cleaner walk into view on the monitor, walk in front of the camera, and empty the room's waste paper basket!

■ Make sure the camera is facing away from the door, so latecomers can come in and sit down with minimum disturbance, and without crossing the camera's view.

Using the camera

■ Don't just use the equipment as set up for you. Adjust the camera setup until you are happy with it.

■ Ideally, have the camera at eye level, looking directly at people, not down at them.

■ If using a long table, have the camera at the end if possible, so the person chairing the videoconference is looking towards the camera as they look at people.

■ Have a monitor as close as possible to the camera. That way, when you look at someone on the monitor, it appears to the camera that you are almost looking them in the eye on the monitor at their end. Eye contact is greatly improved by this.

■ Practise and make yourself familiar with the equipment, and have backup or technical support at hand if necessary.

Communicating on camera

- Vary your voice more than usual, as a lot of the body language and gesture meaning is lost or delayed on screen.
- Move slowly. The camera does not record rapid gestures or movements easily, so make slow movements with your hands if necessary.
- Avoid fidgeting such as tapping, swaying from side to side, smoothing hair etc. – they are amplified and more distracting on camera. To keep still if you really have trouble with this, just imagine you are reading the news!
- Dress carefully. Avoid patterns like houndstooth, paisley or print, and narrow stripes. Green, red and yellow can all throw colours off balance and affect the overall impression.

Using slides or PowerPoint

- This needs to be 36 point minimum font size, or it will be un-readable on the screen at the other end.
- Avoid crowding slides.
- Avoid bright colours – black and white, blue or grey are best.
- Try using just headings or bullet points and talking round them.

Streaming technology

Webcast and similar technologies make videoconferencing available to people without videoconferencing equipment. They can use the Internet instead to broadcast meetings.

> *'Videoconferences need a little care to get right, but with attention to detail they can be highly effective.'*

4 · INTERNET OR WEB CONFERENCING

As we have already said, the Internet has given us a new alternative to meetings – virtual meetings. A virtual meeting room is accessed via a web browser on computers. Web conferencing can offer:

- visuals that can be annotated on-screen
- text-based chat
- live audio
- the ability to work on documents as a group.

Scheduling web conferences

Setting up a web conference is often as simple as going to the service's web site and filling out a form with:

- the meeting time
- attendees
- other details.

The service will usually automatically issue email invitations to all individuals on the list, reducing administrative work for you. There is usually no special software to download, either for the chairperson/organiser or the participant.

Visuals

During the meeting, all parties can see the desired document, spreadsheet, presentation, drawing, online software demo or other visual on their screens at the same time.

Better service providers offer the ability to highlight or underline key ideas or features – just as in a live presentation – and different people can take control as desired. Collaboration capabilities may be available – this is when changes can be made to a document online while everyone watches. Some systems also support broadcast video.

Audio

At its most basic, web conferencing can be combined with telephone conferencing. Most services also offer chat capabilities for text-based interaction, and the most sophisticated systems offer the ability to speak over the Internet through users' computer speakers and a plug-in software utility such as RealPlayer. This is known as VOIP (Voice Over Internet Protocol).

Online questions

Some web conferencing services offer the ability to ask questions of participants at any time and instantly publish the results. This makes immediate feedback possible without requiring discussion – rather like a secret ballot. This can be valuable if you want to gauge reactions or opinions to contentious issues – and is the equivalent of a 'show of hands' to indicate support or not, without anyone knowing which way you vote.

Reporting and archiving

Some service providers permit presentations, documents, annotations, chat and other elements to be archived for future reference. Some can also generate reports indicating who attended, how long they participated, when they departed, and so on – very useful for large meetings.

Costs

Web meetings can cost relatively little, and it usually costs the same whether you meet for one hour or six hours – you pay for access, often on a per head basis.

Hints and tips for web conferencing

■ Keep things simple at first until you are used to the technology.

■ Keep the usual meeting rules – send an agenda and other information, have breaks, don't make the meeting too long etc.

■ Make a fast introduction – then get on with the meeting. Don't let the novelty value distract people for too long at the beginning.

- Check the technology compatibility first. Most service providers provide web pages to check the participants computers first. Get all participants to complete this in advance.

- Plan ahead when using any fancy software or application demonstrations, and have a test run first, to check all will go smoothly on the day.

Advantages of web conferencing

- Eliminates the need to travel.
- Access to a huge potential audience.
- The ability to let people view the presentation later easily if they miss it.
- Interaction.

Disadvantages

- Converted presentations may end up a little worse for wear when viewed on the web.

- Some transitions and animations won't work on some browsers.

- With only 256 colours (216 if both Internet Explorer and Netscape Navigator are being used) your photos may come out blurred and pixilated.

- Sound effects may not translate unless viewers download an audio plug-in (such as RealPlayer).

- Your file size will probably be huge.

- Your presentation may be very slow.

- Attention spans will be a lot shorter – in the privacy of their own offices, attendees will be more likely to write emails, gaze out the window or distract themselves.

'Web conferencing isn't without it's difficulties, but it can often be smooth and impressive. Use it effectively.'

IN SUMMARY

■ Use simple technology solutions to improve your meeting effectiveness.

■ Remember that teleconferencing can be difficult, as purely verbal communication is not necessarily a very effective communication tool.

■ Videoconferencing can only be effective if you use it well. Learn the techniques and do's and don'ts for effective videoconferences.

■ Web conferencing is actually easier than most people think and very effective. Invest time and effort in exploring how to do it properly before using it, however.